Freedom Now!
The Function of Jazz
in the
Civil Rights Movement

by
Christa R. Gammage

Table of Contents

Introduction

Growing up, I have always been surrounded by music. The radio is always on in my home, and there is a never-ending stream of all kinds of music playing through the house unless we are asleep. When I was younger, I did not bother to pay much attention to exactly *what* was playing, but as I got older, I realized that more often than not this music was coming from a jazz radio station. My parents constantly played jazz on the televisions throughout the house, and it served as the background soundtrack to my life throughout high school. It was always a pleasant moment to open my front door and hear the notes of John Coltrane or Art Blakey floating through the air to welcome me home. The Music Choice stations would have information available about the song, which album and which artist it came from, as well as random facts about the artist. I have many fond memories with my family that are accentuated by the sounds of jazz over the late twentieth century.

By the time I was 17, I had played piano for almost ten years. Although I was passionate about the instrument, I sorely lacked a very important skill of playing it—sight reading. Whereas someone of my years of experience should have been able to merely look at a page of music and play it, similar to reading a book, I struggled with this immensely. It would take me minutes to figure out a single note, let alone a chord progression. Walking down the street by my home in

New York City, I saw a sign advertising drum lessons at a reasonable price. Realizing I had struggled to read the notes of piano music, but found strength in reading the rhythms, I decided to give drumming a try. To my surprise, I greatly enjoyed it. It also exposed me to playing all new genres of music; on piano, my teachers had limited me to classical music, but drums showed me an entirely new side to playing, branching out into not only Jazz but Rock, Country, Latin, Afro-Cuban, and Brazilian beats as well.

The summer after high school, I enrolled myself in a program at the New York Jazz Academy. Each day consisted of music lessons, group ensemble, and jazz history talks that enlightened me about the history of the genre. I learned about the legendary drummers, trumpetists, saxophonists, and others that helped contribute to this uniquely American art form and influenced what it has become today. This was my first exposure to the genre's history, and I was fascinated.

When I entered college in the fall, I made sure to continue my music studies with Bard's music department and took weekly private lessons the entire first year. I learned the various beats that defined cultures, from Afro-Cuban to Brazilian, and last but not least, jazz. However, since the drums are an accompanying instrument, it was only a matter of time until I would need to push myself to play with other musicians. By my junior year, I felt ready to join an ensemble with my peers.

That semester, I immersed myself in the music. I was also taking a class on jazz history, and learning about the different stages of jazz over the course of the twentieth century is what initially spiked my interest in the subject. I had never taken a course on music history before, and as an American studies major who was deeply passionate about music I immediately felt this was the topic for me. Simultaneously, I was also taking a class on the history of social movements in twentieth century America. I chose to focus on rock and roll in the Hippie movement of the late 1960s. The class, in conjunction with my jazz history class, made me realize just how great an impact music could have on a social movement. Not only could the music itself be an expression of social values, but it could also bring together groups of people of similar ideologies to convene and reflect upon these values.

The second half of junior year, I spent abroad at King's College London. As an American Studies major, many of the classes I chose to take abroad were about American culture, just from a foreign perspective. The history class I took, Political Culture, Faith, and Belonging in post-1945 United States, gave me a new lens through which to view American history. While my classmates were a mix of American, British, and other nationalities, one thing I did noticed stuck out to me the most: in the class, those not from America constantly brought up racism. Racism was what seemed to characterize American culture in the twentieth century as perceived by foreigners. It was striking to me that in spite of the many accomplishments and engagements that had been undertaken between the United States and Britain in the twentieth century, the topic of central interest to my British peers almost always seemed to be the question of racism and prejudice in the United States.

When it was time to return to Bard my senior year, I was seemingly lost on choosing a topic for my Senior Project. But my interests made me realize a topic that seemed to be staring me in the face: jazz music! The next question was how to relate this to a social movement, as I had similarly enjoyed learning about the influence of Rock music on the Hippie movement. Jazz is a rather new musical genre, compared to others. In my jazz history class at Bard, we spoke at great lengths about the bebop era and how this jazz form was revolutionary in nature. It began to emerge around the mid-1950s through the 1960s, which happened to coincide with the Civil Rights movement. Additionally, many of the jazz musicians of this period were African-American. After having been abroad for a semester, visiting multiple iconic jazz clubs in Paris, and realizing the strong reputation of Americans of the twentieth century as racist from my history class, I came to the conclusion that jazz must have held a rather important part in the Civil Rights movement.

When I began this project, I was not quite sure where to start searching for a definitive question and found an interesting contrast in something that related to my American history class in Britain—although racism was still rampant in the United States, African-Americans being delegated to second-class citizenship, the United States government nevertheless sponsored Black artists to represent the country as a tactic of Cold War diplomacy? It was here that I recognized the importance of this story and just how much irony was behind the U.S. Jazz Ambassador tours. I began to

4

question what influence these jazz musicians held abroad, whether they were vocal about their experience with racial prejudice, and also whether they were vocal about these experiences when they returned to the United States. My experience in London gave me the opportunity to view United States history from a foreigner's perspective, which made me question my own. I realized there was much more to learn on the topic, and began to delve deeper.

As I began to research, I found that there was much more to this topic than I had realized. I began to read Thelonious Monk's biography, *Thelonious Monk: The Life and Times of an American Original* by Robin D.G. Kelley, and soon discovered that many jazz artists of the era were involved in the struggle for racial equality. I also found that some were more involved than others—Thelonious Monk was portrayed as a rather apolitical artist, whereas Louis Armstrong was crowned by the government as a U.S. Jazz Ambassador. *Satchmo Blows Up the World: Jazz Ambassadors Play the Cold War* by Penny M. Von Eschen became a useful source in analyzing jazz abroad, while *Freedom Sounds: Civil Rights Call Out to Jazz and Africa* by Ingrid Monson was practically an encyclopedia for the function of jazz at home. Along with various other sources to support my argument, these came together to create a project that analyzed a musical genre that has, since the mid-twentieth century, largely fallen out of popular favor. Jazz today is seen more as an art music, but still holds great significance in a historical context. Using these texts, I was able to understand this significance in terms of the Civil Rights movement, including analyzing specific musicians, such as Thelonious Monk and Louis Armstrong, in comparison to others, such as Max Roach.

Lastly, I wanted to analyze a specific musical piece in order to support my argument. Through my research, I noticed which jazz musicians were active political players, and which preferred to remain out of the spotlight. One of the most notable jazz activists was drummer Max Roach. He and his wife, singer Abbey Lincoln, had even produced an album by the name of *We Insist! Freedom Now Suite*, that was comprised of five songs relating to their understanding of freedom in the Civil Rights movement. After listening to the album, I realized I had found my perfect content. The album was moving, artfully created, and had a multitude of purpose stemming from each song's composition. Thinking about this specific performance in correlation with the texts I had read, I was impressed to learn just how greatly jazz musicians felt their music could influence their world and racial prejudice.

Ultimately, the project came to be due to a variety of factors. I feel that my personal experience with music in my life is what originally led me in this direction, but it was with the help of my professors around the world that helped me understand that there was much more history behind jazz that solely a new genre. The music held significance to a community that struggled for equal rights in America for hundreds of years. It is a result of the many cultures that came together over the course of the centuries with individual musical notations that, over time, came to be jazz today. As America's classical music, it is important to recognize the place jazz holds in, not only America's musical history, but social and political history as well.

Chapter One:
Activism at Home

On August 7, 1960, New York's Village Gate held the first of many concerts pertaining to the Congress for Racial Equality's "Jazz Sits In" series.1 Such concerts were common in the struggle for racial equality, as they helped raise money for the cause and also allowed for people of the African-American community to gather themselves in support. This particular event was only the beginning of a long stream of benefit concerts to take place over the next few years and sets the scene of the relationship between jazz and the burgeoning Civil Rights movement. Jazz music enabled many of its musicians to enjoy a greater sense of authority in the African-American community over the Civil Rights movement as they grew in popularity in the public eye.

These artists used their music in an attempt to bring greater attention to the race issue in America. Many created musical pieces to express their support, and used their talents to help promote Civil Rights organizations, such as the Congress of Racial Equality and Student Nonviolent Coordinating Committee, among others. The contribution of jazz to the Civil Rights movement was considered controversial in America because of the long and tumultuous history of race relations in the nation, but many jazz musicians, such as Max Roach, Thelonious Monk, Miles Davis, John Coltrane, amongst many others, embraced the music of their culture to show pride in the movement towards racial equality. They faced intense discrimination in their home country as many experienced explicit racism, from being banned from staying in conveniently located hotels on tour to not being able to participate in live radio broadcasts2. Overall, racism greatly limited jazz music on the radio and decreased record sales, but many artists still sought to overcome this issue and spread their views on inequality in the United States. They used their music to promote freedom and raise awareness of the detrimental effects of racism.

Jazz musicians of color faced great discrimination in their own industry. These practices, such as the cabaret card and other tactics of police brutality, inevitably shaped the lives of these musicians and the music they created; ironically Jim Crow had ultimately helped to fabricate the genre and its audiences3. Jazz audiences, originally comprising of exclusively African-Americans and moving into more interracial territory over the course of the 20th century, could not ignore the racialized aspect of the music. Musicians of this era constantly faced racial prejudice, which made traveling for shows increasingly difficult. Hotel rooms were hard to come by, they had "difficulties in procuring food, and lack of toilet facilities on the road. Musicians stayed in boarding houses or private homes in the Black community, slept on the bus or in cars, ate take-out food,... and usually went into the theater from the back."4 In some instances, establishments would not even allow their musicians to dine in the same restaurant in which they were performing. Additionally, even if a musician were able to afford a hotel, many of the them were for only for Whites, forcing musicians to outsource in terms of where they may rest for the night.5 This is particularly evident in looking at the Negro Motorists Green Book. The Green Book, a brochure for the traveling African-American, listed establishments in each U.S. state as well as abroad that would accept them as a guest. The majority of the establishments in the United States were on the lower-class end of hospitality, whereas establishments abroad could be as high-end as 5 stars, such as the Hotel Elysee-Park in Paris.6 This also is a commentary on the differing attitudes towards African-Americans at home versus abroad.

However, discrimination was not only limited to the traveling musician. New York City, beginning in 1940, was popular hub for jazz performers who faced blatant racism by the authorities. The police fingerprinted "every performer at licensed cabarets, issuing identity cards that were denied to 'people they thought were not of good character.'"7 This statute led many famous musicians, such as Thelonious Monk, Miles Davis, and Billie Holiday, to be out of work for extended periods. Although this policy was intended to regulate the general disorderly conduct surrounding the world of jazz clubs in the 1940s and its audiences, it was most definitely highly influenced by racial prejudice when actually implemented. The "cabaret card" ultimately helped to bolster job competitiveness and and musicians' desire for a defined culture of bebop.8

On the other hand, while it was not unusual for White musicians to play with Black musicians in a

Black venue, it was when Black musicians attempted to mix with White performers in White venues that resulted in controversy.9 The mounting dissatisfaction of Black performers in the jazz industry often ended up with angry feelings being placed on a particular White individual, usually the White bandmate or club owner. Due to the economic forces of racism, it was unlikely that an African-American would be able to open his own club or afford many of the opportunities White musicians could pursue. Of course, these feelings of "structural anger" were personalized for someone who could only be partially responsible for a much larger problem in the world. However, such feelings and conversations forced non-African-Americans to confront the racism of jazz by witnessing the racism faced by their counterparts first hand. Many of the White musicians who experienced this either slipped into a defensive "discourse of reverse racism," or came out on the other side with a stronger ability to identify with their African American counterparts in the jazz community and the "sense of togetherness the jazz world offered."10 Furthermore, the persisting ideology of "colorblindness" in jazz failed to address the strength and alteration of racial boundaries in the postwar world. Although interracial harmony did occur on the stage, structural racism endured after the performances were over.11 Nonetheless, some Black performers chose to make light of such racism. For example, when Thelonious Monk reflected upon how whites continuously called Blacks "boys," to which one could take offense, he said: "Ain't no drag... 'cause everybody wants to be young."12 This did not imply by any means

11

that he did not care about racial inequality, rather, musicians such as Thelonious Monk chose to look at the race issue from a slightly different perspective, proving that not all musicians were so as blatantly outspoken when it came to racial issues.

Musicianship was highly influenced by racial inequality, from record contracts to travel and the racial makeup of bands. Such influences ultimately constructed the politics of jazz as the "debates about segregated locals, integrated bands, and mixed audiences took on heightened moral overtones."13 Although many performers felt that the state of race politics in jazz was much further along than that of America society at large, musicians often took note of each other's attitudes both on and off the stage.14 Unfortunately, this made it extremely difficult to enter into mainstream American society on one's own terms. Bandmates were judgmental of each others attitudes towards racism and how one handle racial prejudice. Whereas one musician may not be as vocal about their stance on segregation, such as Thelonious Monk, another musician who is publicly vocal about segregation, such as Max Roach, may feel that any quieter approach was cowardly.

"Local cultural reference" only further separated societal groups, and jazz musicians of the Civil Rights era recognized this separation and sought to make it more relevant—but this only added to how strongly one's commitment to this notion may be evaluated by others.15 How the individual viewed race relations often depended on their experience with racism, and some artists experienced more than others based on

12

their age and location. Thus, an attempt to make the individual experience more relevant would inevitably further separate the individual from the experience of the group. That is, if one were representing the experience of the minority. For example, as race relations improved over the 20th century, some of the older jazz musicians, who had experienced more racist tendencies solely due to having been alive longer, may have a different understanding of how to approach racism than their younger peers. If there were only one older musician in the band, his peers may have differing views on how to combat racism and judge the older musician's tactics if they are not in line with the tactics of his or her peers.

Beginning in the 1940s, Black musicians began to understand, through the stresses of war, the "*worth* of the country, the society, which it was supposed to call its own," and the vital aspects necessary for a happy life this society lacked.16 After World War II, Black soldiers returned home and experience unabated racism. The effort of the Double Victory campaign (freedom abroad but at home as well) had yet to prove victorious, and African-Americans suffered the most in the destabilization of housing and employment in the immediate post-war world as they were typically 'first fired, last hired."17 Thelonious Monk spoke openly about his experience with racial prejudice exhibited in the law enforcement:

The police bothers you more in the United States than they do anywhere else. The police heckle the people more in the United States than they do anyplace else. You don't have as much trouble with the police in no other country like you do in the United States. The police just mess with you in the United States for nothing. They just bully people. They don't do that in no other country but the United States. They carry guns, too. And they shoot people for nothing.[1]

Monk illustrates that he recognizes the unfair treatment of African-Americans by the American police. He points out that he feels this prejudice is worse in the United States than anywhere else, and that it seems to have no legitimate root cause other than one based on race. Experiences such as this could stifle an individual to lose hope in making a change. It also could make one lose hope and trust in law enforcement. As Monk became a more prominent jazz figure, his personal opinions about the police may have influenced his reasons for taking a milder approach to fighting racism.

Furthermore, Miles Davis also had a similar experience with the police. He is recorded as telling a story from August 26, 1959 about an unfortunate situation he experienced outside one of his performances:

I had just finished doing an Armed Forces Day, you know Voice of America and all that bullshit. I had just walked this pretty white girl named Judy out to get a cab. She got in the cab, and I'm standing there in front of Birdland wringing wet because it's a hot, steaming muggy night in August. This white policeman comes up to me and tells me to move on. At the time I was doing a lot of boxing so I thought to myself, I ought to hit this motherfucker because I knew what he was doing. But instead I said, 'Move on, for what? I'm working downstairs. That's my name up there, Miles

14

Davis,' and I pointed up to my name on the marquee all up in lights. He said, 'I don't care where you work, I said move on! If you don't move on I'm going to arrest you.' I just looked at his face real straight and hard, and I didn't move. Then he said, 'You're under arrest!19

Davis' experience was by no means unique. Such unfair practices of the police could most definitely incite a feeling of resentment and anger towards law enforcement. On the other hand, it could also inspire an individual to fight against these tactics. Davis' reluctance to move at the unfair request of the policeman shows his effort to take a stance for himself and African-Americans at large against police brutality. Pointing to his name in lights, Davis clearly illustrates an understanding of his fame and how to use it in order to help fight racial prejudice and police brutality.

The police practiced discriminatory policies, but this racism was not only evident in the streets. Racial prejudice also took place inside the jazz clubs. 52nd Street in New York City had become a hub of famous jazz clubs during the Civil Rights period, which Miles Davis described as a time of "unbelievable" musical progress but also as "real racist." He was often critical of the way he felt Louis Armstrong and Dizzy Gillespie would "laugh and grin for the [White] audience,' and [he] refuse[d] to 'sell out [his] principles' in the same way."20 His unwillingness to compromise his political stance for popularity exemplifies the multitude of feelings surrounding the subject. Davis is an example of the bandmate who judges others for how they choose to engage in the Civil Rights movement. On the other hand, some musicians felt it to be of greater benefit to navigate such situations with a more lighthearted attitude. For example, at a gig of Thelonious Monk's, the band was experiencing explicit racism and Monk instead chose to make light of the uncomfortable circumstances. His bandmate Al McKibbon recalled:

We played in a bar where the owner was prejudiced as hell, man. He just hated blacks, you know. He had a big easy chair behind the bar that was his private chair, he sat in it. Every intermission, Monk would go and sit in that chair. [laughter] It'd break me up. He'd just sit there and smile. And steam would be coming out of the guy's ears.21

Although both Miles Davis and Thelonious Monk had a point in their reaction to the racism they experienced at gigs, it is also important to recognize the role of Gillespie's approach: bebop was considered an aggressive stance of Black culture to many White critics, so Gillespie's more subtle efforts helped to popularize the genre and to counter the more eccentric behavior of musicians such as Thelonious Monk.22 Gillespie recognized the importance of balancing the image of the African-American in the public eye—one that must not appear too eccentric for their White counterparts to identify with. All of these strategies, from Davis' to Monk's to Gillespie's, ultimately helped these artists navigate the difficult terrain of musical innovation and race relations.

As riots appeared on the street to battle the unfair prejudice of racial inequality that permeated the nation, jazz reflected this change as it established a "new" music in the form of bebop.23 Bebop illustrated an effort of African-Americans to separate themselves from the notion that Black Americans were merely an "invention of white Americans."24 The music was the re-creation and redefinition of the alienation of African-Americans in America over the past centuries, but finally on their own terms.25 Jazz of the Civil Rights era represented a "redefining of the canons of value," which took previously undervalued music and forced America to pay attention.26 It exemplified the resistance of African-Americans to dominant White America by creating a genre so revolutionary in essence they could not ignore its genius. The music itself is arguably universal, open to any who practices it, masters its improvisational aspects for creation, and embraces its tones of individuality and ingenuity. But it is impossible to separate jazz from its African-American heritage and its most important components rooted in "the blues and that elusive rhythmic flow called swing."27 The "othering" felt by African-Americans came to exemplify itself in jazz, as artistically it embraced "innovation, invention and change" in music that reflected the "power, exclusion and privilege" occurring in America during this period.28

Moreover, racism in jazz extended into the press as well. Although jazz musicians were primarily Black, their critics were primarily White. This racism is most evident in one of music critic Barry Farrell's pieces in *Time* magazine about Thelonious Monk. As he wrote for one for the most iconic magazines in America at the time, his stories often made the cover and had great influence over the public's imagination. He implied that Monk was a "'good guy' because he [was] not caught up in the 'racial woes [that] are at the heart of much bad behavior in jazz."29 In this critique he is referring to a previous editorial in *Time* magazine that criticized the effects of "Crow Jim" in jazz, stating that Black jazz artists often criticized White jazz musicians for "exploiting 'their music' and employed jazz as a vehicle for Black protest."30 Many White critics presented to the masses a skewed image of the ultimate jazz performer—one that did not participate in racial politics but simply followed the aesthetics and artistry of the form. Additionally, this editorial implied that Monk was a thoroughly apolitical artist and that this was as worthy of recognition as his playing skill. Unlike what this article put forth, though, the urgency and importance of the Civil Rights movement actually encouraged otherwise apolitical artists to involve themselves in the movement in a variety of ways that I will discuss later.

Farrell's article on Thelonious Monk compelled many of its African-American readers to view the article through the lens of racial politics. Monk was presented as rather odd, and perhaps not in the most positive light. The article was in turn received with controversy by the Black community for its eccentric representation of one of bebop's finest musicians. Some felt the article to be authentic and to highlight the forces that helped construct the musician's personality, whereas others challenged its characterization of Monk as classic stereotyping.31 Critic Ralph J. Gleason, a founding editor of *Rolling Stone Magazine*, referred to the article as "revolting" and "libelous to jazz," insisting that *Time* had presented Monk as a "symbol of the native genius... sweaty and bizarre, so as not to ruffle the

18

preconceptions of *Time* thought."32 Furthermore, music journalist Leonard Feather felt that the essay presented the jazz musician as "both drug-addicted and a down-ish buffoon donning a funny hat,"33 which would not help the image of the African-American in America's public eye. Black nationalists and the like felt the article was a blatant attack on one of their "combatants." Writer Theodore Pontifler, who published in the Harlem-based *Liberator* magazine, leveled a harsh criticism at the implications of Farrell's article, claiming that it "warns white America that in the days of talking integration and on the fatal eve of passing a watered-down civil rights bill, they should remember that it could mean more of their daughters will be bringing home an occasional Black genius."34

However, not all critics felt the editorial to be particularly libelous. Writer Ralph de Toledano, critic for the *National Review*, actually praised Monk for his separation of music and politics. He claimed, "Like most of the best jazzmen... he doesn't believe that he must make his art a sledge hammer to pound away at political themes."35 On the other hand, Toledano's critique continued to explore the racialized idea that jazz was more "physical and emotional than cerebral."36 He went on to criticize Monk for being *too* reflexive, and not tapping into his "soul" and removing "dance" from his compositions. Thus, Monk was praised for not being overly Black in a political sense yet simultaneously was chided for not being Black enough in his music.37 Monk and his contemporaries were upset by the article, but there was not much he could do about the publication. Unfortunately, the price of political outspokenness could often be very high, as many jazz artists could see directly. Monk's quiet political stance contrasts with that of Abbey Lincoln or Max Roach, who often found it difficult to obtain musical contracts due to their active political outcries. They were considered "difficult" by the industry, and faced economic decline as a result. It was not until such protests became more socially acceptable, in the years immediately leading up to the passage of the Civil Rights bill, that many musicians felt comfortable to associate themselves with the movement.38

Despite these challenges and policed boundaries, jazz could also serve as a means for integration as well. Jazz was most definitely not a genre solely dominated by Black musicians; the bandstand was constituted of musicians from both White and Black racial backgrounds, establishing "a futuristic social force in which one was finally judged purely on the basis of one's individual ability."39 Beginning with the big swing bands of the 1930s, such as Benny Goodman's, Black musicians were hired into integrated bands. Many Black musicians viewed such integration as a "raiding" of their most valuable musicians.40 However, with the increasing integration occurring in the genre, it was necessary for musicians of both colors to reflect on how jazz created an open space for communication and self-expression.41 In fact, the "colorblind" discourse of such a phenomenon claimed that the ability to play jazz was indeed something that could be divorced from any color at all.42 This ideology was particularly controversial, as many African-Americans were proud of the Blackness found in jazz and did not agree that it was possible to detach the genre from its heritage. As White musicians such as Dave Brubeck and Benny Goodman found favor with the American public, Black musicians often resented the fact that they found such success in a cultural practice that was not their own.

The integration found in jazz at this time could be considered the forerunner of the Civil Rights movement: a glimpse into the possibilities that awaited the melting pot that is the United States. Jazz trumpeter Red Rodney is quoted as saying:

The blacks have always been the forefront of jazz. They've always been the greatest on each respective instrument.... And as far as the white jazz musician, this was the one area in American life where there was honestly and sincerely no prejudice whatsoever. Nothing. We lived together. Ate together. Thought together. Felt together. And it was really the only area in American life where this happened.43

Rodney explains his feelings that the music takes on importance above all else in jazz—including race. The experience of playing with other musicians, regardless of whether they are Black or White, proved that common ground could be found between the races. Black jazz musicians found solace in their expertise in an area not dominated by the White majority. This dynamic made jazz a unique space for musicians to be judged by more than solely the color of their skin.

The jazz industry was truly unique in this sense as it served as a precursor to the integration sought after in the Civil Rights movement. By the 1950s, this notion of integration in the industry had become normalized. It was necessary, for the sake of the future of the music, to oppose segregation on both sides of the color line. Jazz ultimately came to represent much more than simply a new form of improvisational music, but one that also brought its music in line with the future endeavors of the Civil Rights movement and country as a whole. It served as a glorified space in terms of its possibilities for true democracy and equality in art and beyond.44

Integrationists often brought this democracy into the physical sphere. For example, the famous Cafe Society in New York's Greenwich Village was created by Barney Josephson, the club's owner, to encourage socialization between the races. Although many of the jazz musicians he booked were Black, Josephson looked to create a nightclub based on the progressive ideas of interracial circulation.45 The nightclubs on 52nd Street in Manhattan also held similar significance. The color line broke down within these clubs in ways that could lead to the natural emergence of friendships between Blacks and Whites. The audience, although perhaps not as progressive, respected such unprejudiced socialization, indicating that jazz could indeed bring people together.46 Another example of such progressive ideologies would be jazz impresario Norman Granz. His series of Jazz at the Philharmonic in Los Angeles sought to fight racial discrimination by moving jazz away from only the nightclub and into the professional concert hall.47 This movement exemplifies that jazz was indeed a true American art form—one to be respected and regarded as high brow musical production. Lastly, integration is most noticeable in the desegregation of the American Federation of Musicians. A labor union formed for instrumental musicians in the United States and Canada founded in 1896, the AFM had sported Jim Crow policies, prioritizing their White members over their Black counterparts, up until the early 1960s. African-Americans faced "exploitation and racial discrimination" in their search for unionization and had to fight for their right to equal membership.48 The desegregation of the union exemplifies how racial prejudice could also influence the economic status of Black musicians and the quality of their everyday lives.

Additionally, jazz, although derived from African-American heritage, was a hit amongst many White people of the day. The Beatnik generation absolutely adored the music of Thelonious Monk and fellow bebop musicians as they frequented many of Monk's shows at New York City's The Five Spot. However, this popularity could be considered controversial. In Norman Mailer's essay, "The White Negro," he outlines an ideology that jazz and the Black musician in general could offer an "alternative model of masculinity in the age of the grey flannel suit, suburbia, and other sterile voices."49 The average lifestyle of American White suburbia that took over the 1950s contrasted jazz music in that it was a pure manifestation of African-American heritage in an increasingly standardized world. The 1950s consisted of a time where the mainstream was basically all one could see in the media. Jazz's "authentic nature," perceived to be from a culture so different from its White listeners, embodied what its White audiences were searching for in their own lives—the idealization of a move away from the falsified mainstream of suburban America towards a "more liberating model of

African American masculinity and style."50 Jazz gave the Beatniks the opportunity to engage in something different from themselves and the environment they grew up in.

Jazz was also used as a political message in the effort towards integration. Its message as a musical style was one of unconventionality, amongst both Black and White musicians alike. Many Black musicians appealed to the idea of being considered "weird" or "deep" and considered their participation in jazz an act of rebellion that highlighted their separation from the White majority.51 How jazz's artists managed to force the music's way into the public sphere was rebellion enough. Consider that the United Nations declared 1960 to be "The Year of Africa," and afterwards invited Thelonious Monk to perform under the U.N. Jazz Society. "The Year of Africa" was proclaimed due to the vast numbers of African countries finally achieving independence, which also coincided with America's movement towards racial equality.52 Tenor saxophonist Sonny Rollins perfectly describes the force with which jazz pushed political boundaries:

Jazz has always been a music of integration. In other words, there were definitely lines where blacks would be and where whites would begin to mix a little bit. I mean, jazz was not just a music; it was a social force in this country, and it was talking about freedom and people enjoying things for what they are and not having to worry about whether they were supposed to be white, black, and all this stuff. Jazz has always been the music that had this kind of spirit. Now I believe for that reason, the people that would push jazz have *not* pushed jazz because that's what jazz means. A lot of times, jazz means no barriers.53

Jazz's symbolic value of democracy and integration, seen in the way the music is presented on the bandstand, encouraged both a global shift towards decolonizations and revitalized national generation and, in the United States, the Civil Rights movement's effort towards racial equality. African-American jazz musicians sought to find the freedom that the music embodied in their everyday lives, and jazz helped to spread this message as it became the epitome of a world with no racial boundaries.

The genre of jazz gave its musicians the power to explore music freely, which they embraced as they associated this with the principles of the Civil Rights movement. Jazz could be used as a metaphor for the freedom that African-Americans were fighting for in the Civil Rights movement. The "jazz savior," a term coined by author Nate Chinen, was meant to deliver whatever society is considered to be lacking at any present time —"cultural esteem... social currency... historical connection... contemporary agency... institutional elevation... street-level energy... renewal... definition... freedom."54 The music of jazz allowed all of its artists to embody these notions for its audiences, as jazz saxophonist Archie Shepp explained:

The Negro musician is a reflection of the Negro people as a social and cultural phenomenon.... His purpose ought to be to liberate American esthetically and socially from its inhumanity. The inhumanity of the white American to the black American as well as the inhumanity of the white American to the white

American is not basic to America and can be exorcised.55

The process in which such an exorcism of inhumanity took place was not uniform. This process was incredibly diverse and oftentimes contradictory, as such a difficult feat cannot always be perfectly cohesive.56 From the early 1940s onwards, jazz musicians constantly challenged musical norms in the same way the Civil Rights movement challenged the racial prejudice of America. The period during World War II and the following decades were especially turbulent due to the effects "Double Victory" campaign, an effort for freedom abroad as well as racial freedom back in the United States.

Jazz served as a means for musicians to bring attention to the magic of such a genre in its ability to bring those across the color line together, but also to highlight the injustice of having to do so in the first place. In Barack Obama's 2016 welcome speech for the White House International Jazz Day Concert, he reflected upon jazz as "perhaps the most honest reflection of who we are as a nation" as it is a symbolic melting pot because of the many heritages that define the African-American. However, Obama also went on to acknowledge the global audience for jazz and the change it has brought about in countries around the world, explaining that "it speaks to something universal about our humanity—the restlessness that stirs in every soul, the desire to create with no boundaries."57 The fact that a United States president of the twenty-first century can openly speak to these aspects of such a genre helps emphasize why jazz was so important to the

Civil Rights movement: because of its ability to bring musicians together across the color line. The term "bebop" itself was created as a "fighting"58 word to describe jazz which truly exemplifies a music with no boundaries. It transcends beyond its musicality and into the political realm to touch millions across the globe with its message.

Many jazz musicians have continued to concur with this ideology that jazz transcends racial boundaries. Jazz trumpeter Booker Little claimed that jazz should focus "on emotional content, on what might be termed humanity in music and the freedom to say all that you want."59 Jazz pianist Vijay Iyer claims that jazz is a "sense of people creating their own reality."60 Jazz is a conception of one's own reality, brought to physicality through music. Jazz musicians have set out to face the odds and open up a dialogue of new possibilities and ways of seeing music and the world.61 The freedom of improvisation in jazz reflects the enabling of its musicians to feel the power of self-determination in each performance. It is in this space where the goals of jazz music meets "real-world aspirations for freedom and justice."62 Jazz musicians were a symbol of these aspirations, "symbolic of strength, stick-to-it-ness, purity... beyond music, beyond jazz."63 The genre potentially has no comparisons in this aspect of the human spirit. Jazz musicians were unique in this nature; they held a special place in the development of racial relations through art. Jazz drummer Max Roach explained that "the music itself has been a blessing. The music has always been kind of a saving grace, among other things, for people...."64 Thelonious Monk stated that "Jazz is America musically. It's all jazz, everywhere...." a sentiment that would later be echoed by Obama's comments about the appeal of the genre and its importance.65 Jazz became an "instrument of racial understanding,"66 providing White audiences with a means of understanding their black counterparts in society. It provided African-Americans with a new level of dignity in music as the achievements of its famed musicians were laid against the background of the Civil Rights movement.67 Each accomplishment of a Black musician could inspire pride in African-American heritage and help garner more support for the Civil Rights struggle.

Jazz provided a way for otherwise apolitical musicians to participate in the movement towards racial equality. Many jazz musicians were actively involved in the Civil Rights movement, but this does not necessarily mean that those who participated in jazz were just naturally more inclined towards political action. Rather, it is the importance of the Civil Rights movement that obliged these artists to take a stand.68 As jazz vocalist Abbey Lincoln reflected, "I think that the artists joined the bandwagon because it makes your work valid. You have to perform, you have to sing or play about something."69 The enormity of Civil Rights, combined with jazz centered in a Black arts tradition, meant that artists had to consciously be involved or remove themselves from the politics of this era. This "culture of commitment"70 permeated throughout the jazz industry, creating an almost peer pressure type situation for jazz musicians to show their support or risk criticism from their peers.

28

Author Ralph Ellison is once quoted as saying: "Protest is an element of all art, though it does not necessarily take the form of speaking for a political or social program."71 Although many jazz musicians were politically active, many were not. There are most definitely a few names that come to mind when one considers the foreground of political activism in jazz during the Civil Rights era, such as Max Roach, and others who seem to have remained in the background, such as Thelonious Monk. The majority of jazz musicians tended to rely on a "common set of discourses (or ideas) that shaped the way disputes were conceived and the way in which various constituencies chose to put their ideas into practice."72 They found themselves to be similarly affected by the power dynamics found in the jazz industry, such as the issues of racial and economic policies.

An era of dramatic change, the culture of the 1960s inspired musicians to reflect upon their duty as artists in order to understand the broader context of their actions.73 During the era of Civil Rights, the Sit-In movement originating in Greensboro, North Carolina, helped shift the general consensus of musicians and audiences alike from jazz as a colorblind genre to one that was Black-dominated on the part of jazz's African-American community. Many of these artists, such as John Coltrane and Max Roach, were focused on "cultural self-determination and the rejection of mainstream American culture" when it came to jazz by the early 1960s.74 African-American jazz musicians believed their music belonged in the top tier of modern music, and were inspired by the Civil Rights movement to take this stance. They felt it important to legitimize jazz in the eyes of the American public in order to highlight the demand of African-Americans to be regarded as full citizens and included in America's promise for equality and justice. In this effort, art transcended into the sphere of politics in order to force the public to recognize African-Americans as a vital and indisputable part of American society.75

Jazz musicians did this in a variety of ways. The music itself reflected the change in political consciousness these artists strove to make apparent. The modernism of "free chord changes, compulsory tonality, timbral orthodoxy, and the obligation to swing"76 illustrated an unconventional approach to music that ultimately signified their objection to the idea of racial inequality. Artists were almost forced to prove to their contemporaries their artistic virtue and dedication to the cause in this "culture of commitment," and felt they must have their music reflect this ideology in order to be respected.77 Their dedication could be considered rebellious in a political sense, as the musicians demanded to be recognized as legitimate as well as equal citizens and artists. However, some felt that it would be most useful to actively engage in an apolitical image to the public in order to further assert their importance in jazz.78 Thelonious Monk exemplifies this trend. Although he was most definitely angered by the police violence and unfair prejudice that governed society, he insisted that his goal was not to make a musical commentary on the maltreatment of black citizens: "I haven't done one of these 'freedom' suites, and I don't intend to. I mean, I don't see the point. I'm not thinking that race thing now; it's not on my mind. Everybody's trying to get me to think it, though, but it doesn't bother me. It only bugs the people who are trying to get me to the think it."79 At a time when the Civil Rights movement pervaded all aspects of one's life, such a quote reflects an artist's active choice to not give in to the pressures of the media. "Bugging" those who try to force him to conform to society's norms was in itself a political act.

Monk also exhibited this behavior in an interview from *Jazz Magazine* conducted in France by journalists Jean Clouzet and Michel Delorme. When Monk was asked, "what role does art play in the movement for racial justice?", he claimed that although he did not see himself as his race but rather as an American in general, this "doesn't prevent me from being aware of all the progress that still needs to be made.... I know my music can help bring people together, and that's what is important. I think that jazz is the thing that has contributed the most to the idea that one day the word 'friendship' may really mean something in the United States."80 Monk placed more value on the influence he could make through his music than through the vocalization of his political stance. This further emphasizes how some musicians may not have been at the forefront of the movement, but still considered themselves to be politically aware and making a change on their own terms.

Duke Ellington had a similar view of how to participate in the movement towards racial equality. By the 1960s, Ellington was was one of the older musicians on the bandstand. Similar to Monk, he was considered rather reserved in his public protest of racism. When presented with the perspective that he was not publicly involved enough, Ellington replied: "People who think that of me have not been listening to our music. For a long time, social protest and pride in the Negro have been our most significant themes in talking about what it is to be a Negro in this country—with jazz being like the kind of man you wouldn't want your daughter to be associated with."81 Ellington viewed jazz to be so rebellious an art form in itself that he did not feel the need to further vocalize his commitment to the cause. His pride in his music was enough, and he felt that this should be enough for others as well.

Jazz functioned as a source of pride in Black culture and identity in the arts that could withstand racial prejudice and the infiltration of Western elements. This brought about a sense of hope in those facing considerable struggles in their fight against racial prejudice. Jazz tenor saxophonist Dexter Gordon recalls:

I really think it was the start of the revolution, the civil-rights movement, in that sense, because that's what the music is talking about. This is all the young generation, a new generation at that time. And they're not satisfied with the shit that's going down. Because they know there should be changes being made. And actually it was a time of change because it was wartime and people were moving back and forth all over the United States and constantly traveling—armies, war jobs, defense jobs. It was a time of great flux. And it was a time of change, and the music was reflecting this. And we were putting our voice into what we thought was about to be the thing.82

The music of the era reflected the high hopes for change that had captured the hearts of the African-American community during this period. Jazz music was not invincible to the changing ideology of American society, and therefore evolved with it in order to remain relevant to its audiences. The advancements that took place in jazz during this era, from big bands to bebop, essentially affirms the dissatisment of the African-American community and how to change this for the future. Jazz pianist Cecil Taylor also agreed with this notion. Taylor believed that the evils of America lay in the materialism that characterized white society. He felt that the African-American approach to music could cure such evils, and ultimately cure the racial prejudice that plagued the United States: "In my music I am searching for a new truth—a truth beyond the money principle—a truth that will make people treat each other like human beings. America needs what the Negro has for survival." 83 Jazz here is represented as a reflection of Black pride and experience in American society; this message can be extended further to the relevance of jazz to the broader American narrative as African-Americans have played a vital role in the formation of the country.

Musicians also responded to the limitations of racism imposed upon them by establishing a number of musicians' organizations in the 1960s in the form of unions to protect the interests of musicians. Whereas some were dedicated to free jazz and others to general artistic expression, most adhered to a level of "commitment to Black nationalist and utopian vision, economic self-determination and collective business practices, education programs for musicians and community members, and political activism."84 The inconsistencies within the jazz industry inspired these musicians to band together in hopes of instilling change. This change was inscribed with feelings of animosity towards the continuous mistreatment of African-Americans in American society, but also pride in the progress of the black freedom movement.85

Such a trend pervaded the jazz industry; this was most noticeable at the esteemed annual Newport Jazz Festival. In 1960, jazz drummer Max Roach and double bassist Charles Mingus boycotted the Newport Jazz Festival and created their own "Newport Rebels Festival," also in Newport, Rhode Island, not too far from the original's location. This act was in protest of producer George Wein's "inclusion of pop singers, the commercialization of the festival, racial inequality in the music business, and the general exploitative conditions jazz musicians endured."86 Roach explained to the press that all proceeds would "go to fight injustices that are plaguing the musician such as the cabaret-card fight, the unemployment tax... we are also trying to prove that the musician can produce, present, and participate himself."87 Jazz musicians felt it was essential they take matters into their own hands and present themselves as a unified front against the unfair practices of the music industry. The alternative Newport Rebels Festival exemplifies the dedication musicians felt towards the effort to overturn unfair industry practices, one that stemmed beyond music and into the political sphere. Their critique of the music industry was based out of personal experience and linked them to a larger narrative in American history.

Furthermore, the economic penalties jazz musicians faced due to racial prejudice further pushed musicians to take a stance against institutional racism. Jazz musicians were at the forefront of the "international avant-garde," and pushed the boundaries of both art and politics as their most creative phase coincided with the Civil rights movement.88 Jazz during the Civil Rights era could be referred to as the "cultural arm of the black liberation struggle"89—a way to keep African-American morale in high spirits during such a tumultuous time. By maintaining an affiliation with the Black community and avoiding appropriation into the mainstream, jazz represented an extension of African-American culture that instilled pride and strength in the masses.

Many of these goals were mutually exclusive, encouraging musicians to act in political accordance with their economic aspirations. Although it is noticeable that there are musicians whose names are consistently listed on the line-ups for benefit concerts for Civil Rights organizations such as CORE and SNCC, it is important to note that just because an artist did not make themself available for these events that they were unaware of the significance of the movement and the part they may play in it. There was an image of the more apolitical artist, such as Thelonious Monk, to be had during the Civil Rights era most definitely, but it is possible that this was greatly highlighted by the culture of commitment to a political cause that defined the 1960s, thus bringing more attention to the apolitical nature of such artists.90

Perhaps the most notable effort of jazz musicians in their protest of racial inequality was their participation in benefit concerts to support various Civil Rights organizations. Between the years of 1960 and 1965, benefit concerts were very popular in the jazz industry to raise money and bring attention to the Civil Rights movement. Various organizations, such as "SNCC, the National Association for the Advancement of Colored People (NAACP), the Southern Christian Leadership Conference (SCLC), and the Congress of Racial Equality (CORE), presented a number of concerts to help bring attention to their purpose and fundraise. Jazz musicians by the likes of Thelonious Monk, Ella Fitzgerald, Miles Davis, Louis Armstrong, Max Roach, Abbey Lincoln, Cannonball Adderley, Count Basie, Duke Ellington, Dizzy Gillespie, Sarah Vaughan, Charles Mingus, Jackie McLean, John Coltrane, Clark Terry, and Dave Brubeck among others all performed in dedication to these organizations at one point or another.

These concerts were politically charged and allowed musicians to show their support for the cause without having to expand their realm of communication outside that of which they were most comfortable—music. They used the importance of jazz as a music of rebellion and freedom to help bring popularity and esteem to the message against racial inequality.91 Additionally, many otherwise apolitical artists, such as Thelonious Monk, used the concerts as an opportunity to express their support by using their talents to help raise money for the cause without having to fully engage in the protests.

This exemplifies that even though they may not have been as politically involved as other musicians, they still found it important to play their part at the risk of being a target for further racial prejudice.

Benefit concerts of the north were a largely a response to the many horrific acts taking place in the south during the Civil Rights era. From the "Greensboro sit-ins, the Freedom Rides of 1961, the Birmingham movement and March on Washington in 1963, [to] the Mississippi voter registration projects of 1964," these benefit concerts connected northern audiences to their southern counterparts.92 Oftentimes, the audience would hear from someone on the front lines of the movement in the south, giving them a more comprehensive idea of what was happening throughout the movement. Furthermore, they allowed for these organizations to capitalize off their affiliations with celebrity jazz performers, such as Max Roach or Abbey Lincoln, and bring more attention to the struggle for racial equality while making both the audience and performers feel as if they were completing their duties.93

Although musicians were paid for participating in these benefits, payment was at a much lower rate than they may usually make during their normal concert series due to the fact that unions required a minimum number of paid musicians to be granted a benefit event. Once this minimum was established, many of the additional musicians would even choose to play for free. Beyond this, many of the musicians would just turn their earnings over to the organizations afterwards anyways.94

These benefit concerts ranged in size, from smaller, club events to larger "gala performances at concert halls and stadiums."95 They allowed for a practical and easy way for musicians to present a form of activism. The concerts gave the public an idea of the political values of these musicians, without the musicians necessarily having to express these values verbally. They felt the music to be political itself, and through it brought further publicity to these organizations and expanded their northern audiences.96 An example of this would be Thelonious Monk's performances in various benefit concerts. Although he rarely made public statements about the brutality experienced on the front lines of Civil Rights activism, his presence at and contribution to various benefit concerts exhibits that he may have found his actions could carry a greater weight in support for the cause than his words.

The Congress for Racial Equality (CORE) was a major player in organizing these benefits. During the Greensboro lunch-counter sit-ins od 1961, CORE gained high national visibility beyond just the south. CORE's community relations director, Marvin Rich, was heavily involved in efforts to publicize the organization and arrange for special fundraising events.97 Rich recalls: "Benefits really began... with the huge increase in publicity after the sit-ins of 1960.... Then people would call us.... Something would happen in the newspaper. People would be indignant. They'd want to do something, and we'd do it."98 The dedication of these organizations to bring activism to the north, where a sit-in would not carry as much weight, was rooted in bringing the same message of integration to a space where they thought it obe just a relevant. Jazz critic Nat Hentoff agreed: "The atmosphere, especially in a place like New York, was very much, 'we've got to do something. We've got to have these benefits. And we've got to do whatever we can.' It was just part of the air."99 The spirit of Black pride and the importance of overcoming racial boundaries was just as effective in the north as in the south. Benefit concerts brought about that spirit in a community atmosphere to show their support for the events occurring in the south.

The Village Gate was a popular New York club that often sponsored events by CORE. The first of these was on August 7, 1960, called "Jazz Sits In," supporting the larger moral statutes concerning the southern Civil Rights movement.100 Participating in this particular event were Thelonious Monk, Clark Terry, Bill Henderson, and Jimmy Giuffre.101 The owners of the Village Gate, Art and Bert D'Lugoff, were particularly supportive of anti-racism and went on to hold a weekly "Cabaret for Freedom" on Sundays, organized by Maya Angelou and Godfrey Cambridge to fundraise for the Southern Christian Leadership Conference (SCLC).102 CORE also held benefits at the famous Five Spot, such as the "Sit In for Freedom," in response to the Birmingham church bombings in 1963, and also at Goodson's Town Cabaret in the bronx.103 The largest of these CORE-sponsored benefit concerts was on June 28, 1961, held on New York's Randall's Island and billed as "Jazz Supports the Freedom Riders."104 With performers such as Louis Armstrong, Gerry Mulligan, and Cannonball Adderley, this event raised money for the cause and also drew audiences to enjoy the music of the movement. A month later, CORE managed to prominently present themselves on live television as they organized a telethon for the Freedom Riders on New York's WNTA channel. The show featured Billy Taylor, Lena Horne, Cal Tjader, Art Blakey, Oscar Brown Jr., and Horace Silver, amongst others, and generated almost $30,000 in revenue.105 This further emphasizes the importance of these concerts for each organization and how they played an important role in bringing racial equality to the attention of both performers and audiences.

Furthermore, the Student Nonviolent Coordinating Committee (SNCC) also participated in the benefit concert trend. Most notable of these concerts would be "A Salute to Southern Students," held at Carnegie Hall on February 1, 1963. The concert was meant to raise money for the organization's growing work in the south, "commemorate the third anniversary of the sit-in movement," and bring attention to the violence these students faced in order to gain the constitutional rights they deserved.106 It was the first SNCC fundraiser to be held in the north, and they managed to raise almost $16,800 and provide food relief to hungry protestors through the event.107 Performers included Thelonious Monk, Charles Mingus, Herbie Mann, and Tony Bennett, as well as the SNCC Freedom singers. Thelonious Monk even went out to dinner afterwards to a nearby restaurant with a few of the SNCC activists to learn more about the organization. Monk later accepted an invitation to join the Friends of SNCC's Sponsoring Artists' Committee, expressing his support despite his otherwise apolitical public reputation.108

Carnegie Hall was also home to another famous jazz benefit. Miles Davis played to benefit the African Research Foundation in 1961; although it was not a Civil Rights organization, Davis participated in part to celebrate African-American cultural pride. The concert is famous for its recording, *Miles Davis at Carnegie Hall*. 109 On the other hand, Miles Davis did play some events for the likes of SNCC, CORE, and NAACP Legal Defense.110 His Lincoln's Birthday concert, on February 12, 1964, benefitted Civil Rights organizations and resulted in two albums: *My Funny Valentine* and *Four & More*.111 Furthermore, the Negro American Labor Council (NALC) also held its own benefit concerts. In August 1963, NALC held a gala benefit for the March on Washington at the Apollo Theater that drew virtually every jazz musician in the city, including Thelonious Monk, Tadd Dameron, Art Blakey, Cozy Cole, Ahmad Jamal, and Clark Terry.112 Beyond jazz, people such as Sidney Poitier, Paul Newman, Archie Moore, and even a young Stevie Wonder attended the event.113

These events would attract wealthier donors by gathering celebrities of both races that gave the events a bourgeois appeal.114Another example of such a bourgeois concert is a benefit that took place in December 1964 for *Freedomways*, "an influential journal devoted to politics, arts, and culture whose first editor was Shirley Graham Du Bois, wife of W.E.B. Du Bois."115 The concert featured John Coltrane, Abbey Lincoln, Max Roach, and Bill Dixon, but also attracted other prominent people by the likes of Martin

41

Luther King Jr., Ossie Davis, Paul Robeson, and Harry Belafonte to come support the cause.116 This exemplifies the strong interest the public had in the Civil Rights struggle and how it came to garner the support of both upper and lower classes.

Jazz music functioned as the soundtrack of the Civil Rights movement in a number of ways: from the nature of the music itself to benefit concerts, jazz gave its musicians the opportunity to protest racism. Jazz's democratic nature makes a statement in itself; the bandstand, over the course of the twentieth century, became a leading space for integration that would eventually permeate the rest of the United States. Its artists recognized this power, and used their celebrity status to support the cause. Musicians such as Max Roach and Abbey Lincoln constructively used their fame to vocalize their opposition to segregation, whereas others, such as Thelonious Monk, were inspired by their peers to involve themselves in the movement despite their more apolitical tendencies. The benefit concerts they participated in were a means for musicians to help raise money for Civil Rights organizations and present themselves as unified against racial prejudice.

Ultimately, jazz reflected the statutes of and helped further the Civil Rights movement in the United States in its integrationary practices and pride in African-American culture, which gave a voice to the many jazz musicians who worked to overcome racism.

Chapter Two:
Activism Abroad

The Civil Rights Movement occurred simultaneously with the Cold War; the latter of which encouraged the United States government to fund a series of cultural tours to prove to the rest of the world the cultivation of the American aestheticism. Ironically enough, the United States Bureau of Educational and Cultural Affairs (CU) decided to sponsor jazz musicians, many of whom were African-American, as ambassadors of highbrow American culture to the rest of the world. Although race relations within the United States were highly contested, the United States government asked these second-class citizens to represent the country's democratic principles abroad despite its lack of such at home. These jazz ambassadors used their assigned position to advertise the flaws of the American democratic system from the view of African-Americans during the most intense time of the Civil Rights movement.

Jazz brought the music of African-Americans to the forefront of the globe's attention during the Cold War. The music made evident that America did not lack an indigenous music—rather, it embraced the amalgam of American culture and the African-American experience that resulted in an art form as unique as jazz. Jazz served to express the democratic ideals of the United States simply in its formation—the creative process, as quoted by jazz drummer Max Roach, is "democratic" in itself: "When a piece is performed, everybody has the opportunity to speak on it, to comment on it through their performance. It's a democratic process."117 However, jazz also functioned as a method for the unification of the diverse peoples of the United States as well as abroad. Its historic basis continuously influenced musicians of all genres, and became an international language that enabled them to express real-world problems in a personal context.118 Ultimately, jazz abroad served as a means to not contain communism, but also to represent the democratic ideals of the United States to the rest of the world, incidentally giving spotlight to the Civil Rights movement and advocacy to the jazz ambassadors who sorely lacked the ability to exercise these ideals within their own country.

The United States government intensely feared the spread of communism, and thus supported sending jazz ambassadors to countries throughout the world that they felt were particularly susceptible to fall into the communist regime. From the mid-1950s to the late 1970s, the federal government sent abroad numerous musicians to where they felt the arm of diplomacy was in order. The State Department sponsored "twenty-eight tours featuring jazz groups" during some of the most crucial years of the civil rights movement, from the mid-1950s to the end of the 1960s.119 Slightly over 50 percent of these tours were headed by African Americans, including "Dizzy Gillespie, Wilbur De Paris, Louis Armstrong, Cozy Cole, Duke Ellington, Earl Hines, Randy Weston, Charles Lloyd, Oliver

44

Nelson, Junior Wells, Buddy Guy, Benny Goodman, Woody Herman, Jack Teagarden, Red Nichols, Charlie Byrd, and Paul Winter."120 With a range of styles, these bands toured the corners of the globe in order to help the United States present a propagandized front of democratic freedom for all United States citizens. These bands additionally added to jazz's international development, laying a foundation for future musicians to construct a global framework that would serve as a base for the future of the art form.121

The United States government utilized the jazz tours as a form of cultural presentation; this presentation was not meant to speak for the realities of American society, but rather to help "shape foreign perceptions of it."122 It was how the United States was viewed by its counterparts abroad, rather than the reality, that was important to the State Department during the tours. The CU chose jazz in an effort to communicate America's core values of "social justice, egalitarianism, and democracy,"123 as well as assert the country's position in the world as a happily multiracial nation in spite of the country's public racial conflict. The attempt of the State Department to forge such an image for the United States in the eyes of other nations was a result of the rise in global freedom movements after World War II; these movements helped establish a coalition of "musicians, supporters of the arts, and liberals in the State Department"124 that saw the value of American culture in the face of diplomacy. The CU appropriated the music of its African-American population as an necessary asset for its anti-communist agenda: a product of intellectual warfare to win the Cold War and defeat the advance of communism.125

State officials argued for the importance of jazz abroad, claiming it enabled communication with various populations that crossed political boundaries. Jazz musicians were instrumental in the correspondence of the United States with the populations of the countries they visited, importantly including "the university students, as well as with the young community leaders and emergent political figures."126 The success and even initial idea of the tours reflected the immense capability of the government's State Department to problem-solve and manipulate any situation to suit them.127 The jazz tours helped to implement the prominence of Black American artists abroad, as well as place emphasis on the importance of the arts in the United States. These jazz ambassadors heavily influenced the countries and the people who experienced their music with their optimistic spirit. Jazz's most immediate objective —"finding common purpose together, through improvisation"—was well-received by international audiences and could be understood and adapted by almost any "local custom or inflection."128

The CU chose jazz as its cultural export due to its reputation as a purely American art form—whereas the Soviet Union and other distinct European countries exported the ballet and opera, America sought to provide contrast with a uniquely American art form. The government felt that jazz most accurately represented the principles of the American democratic system. Each "jam session is a miniature democracy.

Every instrument is on its own and equal. The binding element is toleration and consideration for other players."129

Thus, it is no surprise that the United States government utilized the opportunity to reclaim jazz as its own trademark cultural export. Jazz truly as a uniquely American art form, one that exclusively reflected the melting pot that is the United States rather than the tradition of European arts, such as classical music.130 The racially integrated bands sent abroad assisted the United States in its "battle for ideological hegemony"131 against the Soviet Union by presenting to the world a united cultural front.

Jazz abroad was not only presented in the form of government funded tours, but also through the radio. The most popular of these being "Willis Conover's daily *Music USA* program on the USIA's Voice of America radio broadcasts."132 By the late 1950s, *Music USA* reached an estimated audience of thirty million in eighty countries.133 Conover himself believed in the importance of jazz as a political entity, describing it as "structurally parallel to the American political system" and "embodying American freedom."134 As one of the most powerfully influential people on the radio, he believed that jazz gave a sense of freedom to those who were denied such freedoms otherwise. This was an effort to make a direct connection between African Americans and the audiences the government chose to target abroad. Conover is quoted as stating: "This is jazz. And this is America. That's what gives this music validity. It is a cultural reflection of the way things happen in America.... People in other countries can feel this element of freedom. They love jazz because they love such freedom."135 Conover's dedication to jazz and striking reputation abroad helped pave the way for the jazz tours and the demonstration of the country's cultural diplomacy.

The jazz ambassadors themselves represented much more to the countries they visited than simply American culture. They made connections for the United States abroad that represented the country's ideals of hope and opportunity, as well as celebrating the individual's importance within a larger collective without implying the "power of empire."136 This highlights the discrepancy between the jazz musician's individual identity and their place as a citizen within a larger nation.137 The instruments and voices of the jazz musicians themselves articulated the ideals of the American society they were familiar with, creating a particular power in jazz for African-American musicians who were oppressed by Jim Crow at home. It brought the African-American experience to the forefront of global attention, particularly the contradictions of American democratic principles and the relegation of African-Americans to second-class citizen status.138

However, the United States government continuously attempted to downplay these allegations in an effort to portray the unrealistic image of jazz as a "colorblind" music. The State Department struggled to depict jazz as a music that remained above race relations—a music seemingly untouched by the violence of the Civil Rights movement that was occuring at home. This is particularly evident in the naming of White jazz musician Benny Goodman as Consulting

Director of Popular Music Programs on Russian Language Broadcasts by the State Department.139 Whereas Dizzy Gillespie, a black jazz musician sponsored by the state, needed to fight for recognition in his cultural achievements, Goodman was readily accepted by the public and firmly believed jazz to be "a completely democratic music" that defied the boundaries of race.140 The government's place in supporting such an ideology shows their dedication to promoting an unrealistic image of race relations in America—one that stood to be much more inclusive than the reality.

Furthermore, the tours also helped create a sense of pride in African-American culture that confronted transnational boundaries. This is noticeable in how one embassy report claimed, in a reflection of the iconic African-American song "Joshua Fit the Battle of Jericho":

The name 'Joshua' can be considered as a real symbol in America where the trumpet of Armstrong, Gillespie, and others has brought forth from the depths of the suffering Negro people the heartrending tones, which under the name of jazz, have caused several walls of racial discrimination to break down.141

Jazz's place in American politics put the music in the forefront of the public imagination, giving the jazz ambassadors greater authority to bring attention to the detrimental effects of segregation. The State Department's commitment to presenting the United States as a unified front ultimately consisted of presenting a nation that had been revolutionized by the Civil Rights movement.142 The jazz musicians sponsored by the tours were called upon to show the "true character" of the United States, one which reflected a world governed by "racial harmony."143 Although the jazz ambassadors were by no means silent about their racial situation at home, each successful tour further alienated the reality of racial tension in the United States as they contributed to the illusion of healthy race relations.

In addition to wanting to project an unrealistic image of American society, the United States government also wanted only to show the world the best of America. This included only sharing jazz that the State Department deemed worthy of representing the country abroad. State officials supported a rather elitist attitude towards American culture, some even believing that it had surpassed the sophistication of European culture. However, this highbrow American culture consisted only of mainstream jazz, not avant-garde or free jazz, which were regarded as "lowbrow music."144 This makes evident the CU's belief of mainstream jazz as embodying the principles of the United States' mission in the Cold War, but also the belief that not all music of African-American heritage may make the cut. This notion faced great opposition in the jazz industry, as they felt that all forms of jazz should be recognized as highbrow.

As mainstream artists felt compelled to seize the State Department's opportunity for "freedom" to travel the world as a jazz ambassador in order reach across boundaries of different countries and peoples, they also felt the need to maintain the integrity of their own notion of "freedom": one which included full participation in their democracy.145 The government shunned free jazz because they felt it too thoroughly "embodied the ideologies of revolutionary and Black cultural nationalism"146 rather than those that the United States wanted associated with its national image. It was often the plight of the African-American in America and the culture surrounding this plight that was found to be so inspiring by groups around the world. Government officials aimed to quell the conversation surrounding these contrasting elements of American culture, which created a discrepancy between the jazz ambassadors and officials in terms of the goals of the tours.147

The jazz ambassadors also struggled to accept a music construed of African heritage as "colorblind." They quickly recognized the irony of representing a nation in which they did not qualify for simple civil liberties, feeling instead that they had been relegated to second-tier citizen status with rights that were constantly under threat. The use of jazz in American diplomacy inevitably advertised American weaknesses, most importantly the Civil Rights movement.148 The jazz musicians that participated in the national tours utilized their voices and instruments to vocalize their aspirations to live in a world where America was no longer governed by the laws of Jim Crow. Louis Armstrong is quoted as saying that he "was still awaiting the day when he would be 'really free,'" at the time of the tours.149 Similarly, Duke Ellington frequently publicly condemned racial segregation in his home country, saying he "hoped the race problem in the United States would soon be resolved in favor of the

Negro."150 Abroad, jazz ambassadors frequently dealt with answering questions regarding the Civil Rights struggle at home. Jazz could not be brought abroad without bringing the Civil Rights struggle with it.

The State Department's mission to export America's most highbrow culture could not come without a price. To export jazz meant to export, in Ellington's words, "an American idiom with African roots"—the Civil Rights movement.151 The jazz tours gave musicians the opportunity to vocalize their opposition to Jim Crow as they gained a spotlight in the public eye. Although this was perhaps not in the best interest of the State Department, it allowed for the projection of Black American exuberance abroad. The celebration of African-American culture around the world gave many jazz musicians increased confidence in their identity, both as a community and as an individual within such community.152 Unfortunately, the State Department also recognized this and how the jazz tours brought greater attention to the racial problems that plagued the United States. After the school desegregation crisis in Little Rock, Arkansas, those that constructed the jazz cultural tours were extremely averse to sending any more Black musicians abroad during the years 1957 to 1960.153 They felt threatened and challenged the efficacy of the tours in fear of what the jazz ambassadors may have had to say about the events leading up to the crisis and the Civil Rights movement.

The United States government was constantly struggling to downplay the severity of the violence against African-Americans that occurred throughout the struggle for racial equality to audiences abroad. The

United States government created a "Cold War paradox: the cultural expression of one of the nation's most oppressed minorities came to symbolize the cultural superiority of American democracy."154 This was the unavoidable result of an effort to prove the rest of the world wrong when it came to American cultural and democratic principles. Especially in the eyes of the Soviet Union, the racism that characterized the United States relegated American culture as depraved, greedy, and selfish. 155 The jazz tours proved as the perfect opportunity to prove these accusations inaccurate. Jazz and the Civil Rights movement had common ideologies in terms of the way quarrels were addressed and how to execute their strategic agenda. For the government to have brought jazz into the public eye further exacerbated the the aspects of the conflict over "race, leadership, strategy, and policy goals" of the Civil Rights movement that fell in line with the "arguments over race, power, aesthetics, and economics" in jazz.156 Jazz musicians were pleased with the recognition of their music as equivalent in stature to European classical music and the American government's embrace of jazz, and felt as though they were slowly breaking down the racial barriers that held them.

However, the advances made through jazz abroad were constantly contrasted with the setbacks following the Civil Rights movement at home. More than any other single event, the church bombing of 1963 in Birmingham, Alabama publicly shamed the United States government in the eyes of the rest of the world. As one Nigerian journalist observed at the time, the United States appeared to be one of "the most barbaric state[s] in the world."157 At the same time as the jazz tours and the Civil Rights struggle, many African nations were rising out of the hands of European colonial control. The fight for the self-determination of many African countries brought into the headlines the brutal violence that was plaguing African-Americans of the United States. After the events in Birmingham, President Kennedy was obligated to declare Civil Rights a "moral crisis" in response to the criticism he received from Prime Minister Milton Obote of Uganda. The Prime Minister had written an open letter to President Kennedy, objecting to the cruel treatment of the protesters in Birmingham. The State Department was aware that the televised conflict of the Civil Rights movement had a "dramatic impact on those abroad who listen to our [the United States'] words about democracy and weigh our actions against those words."158 President Kennedy officially declared the Civil Rights struggle a "moral crisis,"159 and jazz musicians watched in awe as the violence ensued, determined to use their place in the public eye for justice.

What influence the State Department lacked at home over the Cold War, it made up for in its endeavors abroad. The United States' cultural exchange program was the effort of the government to gain the "'P' factor—the 'psychological dimension of power."160 The Cold War called for the United States to communicate an affinity for "healthy race relations and the sanctity of civil liberties," despite the fact that the United States often did not meet these standards.161 In order to foster the idea that these values were a reality in America, it made sense for the State Department to appropriate African-American culture. Officials determined that the democratic atmosphere found in America harbored the necessary environment for such creativity, which was ultimately a reflection of America's cultural vitality.162 Including jazz in the cultural tours served as a means to lessen the criticism about America's "cultural and racial identity."163 It enabled America to present itself as integrated and modernist in the same manner as its Soviet counterparts. As a result, the image of racial equality and integration became symbol of American democracy to audiences abroad.

On the other hand, it was evident in the media that the struggle for racial equality was by no means solved by the early 1960s. African-American musicians such as Dizzy Gillespie, Louis Armstrong, Miles Davis, Ornette Coleman, and Duke Ellington used the tours to vocalize the struggles of African-American peoples back home. They used the tours to legitimize the music of African-American culture and place the "demand for full citizenship and inclusion in modernity's promise of equality and justice for all" in the public spotlight of audiences abroad.164 The cultural tours forced jazz into the good graces of mainstream American culture, alongside the image of tense race relations.

The jazz musicians on these tours were determined to remind the American public that jazz was a music of African-American heritage that refused to face complete appropriation. Conflicts that occurred throughout the tours, such as for whom they were meant for, musicians preferring to engage with local musicians rather than attend official functions, and musicians perseverance in placing their own unique signature on American diplomacy, illustrate these musicians dedication to "project a cultural statement and musical expression that constituted 'something more than the American idiom.'"165 Jazz musicians sought to use the tours as an opportunity to embrace their position on the civil rights struggle, but also to prove that African-American music had something to offer the world.

Jazz was a music of America's melting pot—a form of cultural exchange that had evolved out of both African and European diaspora.166 The music represented the freedom African-Americans had attained after slavery and still struggled to attain.

Furthermore, jazz served as a "cultural translator"167 for the African-American people at home and those lacking basic freedoms abroad. Whereas many African-American musicians on the tours were held back by Jim Crow laws at home, they found they had a profound influence over the the presentation of Black people and their culture on audiences at home and abroad.168 Perhaps to the dismay of the State Department, the jazz ambassadors were by no means quiet about their opinions of Jim Crow segregation. As Dizzy Gillespie recalled, "I sort've liked the idea of representing America, but I wasn't going over to apologize for the racist policies of America... I know what they've done to us, and I'm not gonna make any excuses."169 Although they were honored to have been selected to participate in the tours by the government, they refused to be forced to publicly support the race politics that

56

characterized the United States.

Musicians felt the goal of the tours were to bring people together in the face of the Cold War, not to downplay the faults of the United States. In their efforts to complete this goal, musicians such as Dizzy Gillespie were eager to meet the people of the foreign countries, engage with local musicians, "hand out free tickets, give away instruments to promising local musicians, and even buy clothes for young fans who sat outside the door of theaters every night to listen but could not afford a ticket."170 Jazz ambassadors valued their position to connect with the people of each nation they visited and made it a priority. They took on the "contradictions of Cold War internationalism"171 by extending a kind hand to those in need and speaking freely about their own needs back in America. They essentially asserted themselves to the State Department to project what aspects of American culture they felt the world needed to understand.

Ultimately, the United States jazz ambassadors during the Civil Rights movement helped bring attention to the their struggle for racial equality at home while they traveled overseas. The irony of the government exporting Black musicians in order to represent American culture abroad serves as a reflection of the tension of racial relations during the twentieth century. However, it also provided ample opportunity for these musicians to speak their mind about the racial tensions they experienced back home. While the government most definitely strategically chose which artists to send abroad, making sure none would reflect poorly on the United States, these artists, such as Louis

57

Armstrong and Dizzy Gillespie, recognized the importance of their position for African-Americans and what publicity they could bring to the cause. Additionally, the tours, with the help of the radio, brought jazz into the forefront of the public eye in new ways. Jazz became a staple of American culture as viewed by foreigners and an ample representation of the democratic principles the United States stood for.

Chapter Three:
Max Roach's
We Insist! Freedom Now Suite

On January 15, 1961, an event sponsored by CORE at New York's Village Gate brought Civil Rights activists to gather in honor of one of the movement's most politically charged jazz works so far.172 Max Roach's *We Insist! Freedom Now Suite*, made in collaboration with his wife and singer, Abbey Lincoln, lyricist Oscar Brown, Jr., drummer Michael Olatunji, and tenor saxophonist Coleman Hawkins, was performed in solidarity with the movement towards racial equality.173 It expressed a need for freedom and individual equality in the United States that still holds relevance today. As artists saw the violence occurring on the front lines of the movement in the south, they felt that their music needed to reflect the experience of the African-American in the context of racism.

The 1960s was an era of immense change in the United States, and the art of the era reflected this. Jazz in the 1960s took on new meaning in terms of Civil Rights and the struggle for racial equality. As a result of the massacres, bombings, and various other horrific acts that plagued the American south, jazz musicians felt an imperative to show the country, through music, how these circumstances have affected them and their fellow African-Americans. Roach's *We Insist!* is a piece emblematic of the struggles faced by African-Americans throughout the centuries.

The *Freedom Now Suite* is meant to communicate the African-American experience. *We Insist!* consists of five songs that bring the listener from the heart of the American south of the Antebellum era to the modern struggle against apartheid taking place place in the 1960s during the album's release.174 It is perhaps one of the most well-known works, other than John Coltrane's 1963 recording of *Alabama*, created during the Civil Rights movement with specific reference to the oppression experienced by African-Americans over the course of American history. The work was played at various benefits concerts, and even the Newport Jazz Festival, over the following few years. The jazz community With explicitly political material, the music takes on a life of its own as it progresses through history in five movements: "Driva' Man," "Freedom Day," "Triptych: Prayer, Protest, Peace," "All Africa," and "Johannesburg."175 Each song represents a different time in the history of African-Americans and has a particular sound to draw the listener in.

The album received mixed reviews. While Civil Rights activists and organizations appreciated its efforts to draw attention to the struggle of African-Americans, others seemed to disagree. For example, after a performance a review for *Variety* claimed that the album had a "bitter mood" and felt that it was "new-frontier club stuff and most likely a little too far out in uncut timber for most tastes."176 However, other audiences seemed to enjoy the piece. Roach and Lincoln went on to perform the set at a multitude of other venues over the next few years. During the summer of 1961, *We Insist!* was performed at the fifty-second annual convention of the NAACP in Philadelphia, Pennsylvania at the Sheraton Hotel. In fact, it was considered so popular that talk of a tour in the fall was discussed, although Lincoln confirms that the tour never actually took place.177 In 1964, Roach went on the perform the work at the prestigious Newport Jazz festival with Lincoln, tenor saxophonist Clifford Jordan, bassist Eddie Kahn, and pianist Lonnie Liston Smith.178 Beyond continuing to publicize the album and its message through live performance, Roach announced in a 1963 *New York Amsterdam* article that the album would be available free of charge to "any fund-raising organization requesting it."179 Roach's dedication to spreading the message of racial equality and how important he felt his music was to the movement is illustrated by his continuous emphasis that proceeds should be donated towards Civil Rights organizations.

The first song of the album, "Driva' Man," depicts a slave terrorized by his master in a cotton field in the deep American south during the Antebellum period. Written from a slave's perspective, the song takes on a work-song type persona.180 The song begins with Lincoln singing a capella between beats played out by a tambourine. Lincoln's words echo between Roach's cymbal play that is meant to represent the noises of rattling chains and whip lashes, a direct commentary on slavery and the need for resistance.181 Hawkins follows afterwards, following Lincoln's words on tenor sax. The music brings the listener back to the harsh reality of slavery and how such brutality was occurring merely a century before.182 The lyrics themselves reflect such brutality:

"*Get to work and root that stump Driva man'll make you jump Better make your hammer ring Driva man'll start to swing*

Ain't but two things on my mind Driva man and quittin' time.'183

The lyrics illustrate to the listener the fear and torture that the slave would experience when "Driva' Man," the slave master, would arrive on the scene. This shows the roots of the need for resistance through the eyes of a slave during America's most devastatingly unequal time for African-Americans. Lincoln's strong voice contrasted against the metronomic cymbals conveys the combative atmosphere present in the plantation fields.

"Driva' Man" is followed by "Freedom Day," a song that illustrates the expectancy and happiness associated with Emancipation Day that took place almost 100 years before the album's release. However, the music also exhibits an almost "non celebration," one that wants to be excited, but also is hesitant and curious for the future.184 The album itself was originally meant to be released as a celebration of the 100 year anniversary of the Emancipation Proclamation. However, due to the rapid progress of the Civil Rights movement, the album's release date was pushed to an earlier date of 1960 rather than 1962. 185 Such wondering about the future after the Emancipation Proclamation perhaps also resonated with the burgeoning Civil Rights movement. Lincoln seems to articulate her disbelief, that is furthered by Roach's upbeat rhythm and followed by solos that can be construed as rather timid.186 This can be interpreted as a sense of having survived thus far, but knowing that an optimistic outlook may lead to disappointment as there is still far to go until complete equality. Lincoln sings about her desire for the passage of a Civil Rights bill to end segregation, giving the album a particularly poignant and modern relevance to it.

The most recognizable song of the album, "Triptych: Prayer/Protest/Peace," follows "Freedom Day" and speaks to the struggle of an oppressed people. The three-part song begins with "Prayer," a duet between Roach and Lincoln where Lincoln sings in an almost gospel-like manner to reflect her prayers for equality.187 Gospel sounds were common in female jazz music, as is also evident in Mahalia Jackson's work. Such sounds evoke a sense of purity in her intentions for the listener and expresses her sincere hope in the future.188 Furthermore, drawing on spiritualism links the song to a long-standing aspect of African-American cultural identity in the United States.189 Lincoln's vocal tones are accompanied by Roach's sporadic drumming in the background. She goes on to explore a large vocal range in "Protest," contrasting the calm of "Prayer" and "Peace," and consists of radical screaming and a much higher paced drum behind it. This brings the listener to imagine a more combative and authoritative form of resistance to oppression, and is the most controversial part of the song.190 The fact that the song does not use words, but rather Lincoln's melodic voice, shows that these emotions can be conveyed without language at all. Each of her screams over frivolous drumming reenact the "rape, witness, passage, horror, murder, [and] protest"191 experienced by African-Americans over the last 100 years and beyond. Lincoln recalls that it was Roach's idea to include the screaming, which convey a sense of suppressed rage towards the oppressor.192 "Peace" comes at the end in an almost haunting and calming emotion in the face of Roach's drums. Lincoln's sighing over the quietness of the drums presents her as almost angelic. Roach explained that "Prayer" can be considered "the feeling of relaxed exhaustion after you've done everything you can to assert yourself. You can rest now because you've worked to be free."193 The song takes the listener on a journey from hope, to despair, and finally to peace in the knowledge that one has done all one can to achieve liberation for oneself and for the African-American community.

The next song on the album, "All Africa," reflects the changing landscape of the African continent during the 1960s. In an era in which many African nations were finally gaining independence from their colonizers, beginning with Ghana in 1957, African-Americans were viewing this African nationalism as inspiration for their own struggle in the United States. Such a struggle had been recognized since the Emancipation Proclamation, and was particularly evident to scholars such as W. E. B. Du Bois who anticipated a global color line being drawn through the imperialism of the early 20th century.194 "All Africa" shows the pride in continental Africa's past and in its imminent future, and the link African-Americans hold to it.195 Nigerian Olatunji uses his polyrhythmic drums in response to Lincoln's vocal introduction in which she chants the names of various African groups. In his native Yoruba dialect, Olatunji responds to Lincoln with a quote about freedom that is associated with each group.196 This serves as a bridge between African-Americans and Africans, showing commonalities between the two groups and a sense of pride in one's heritage.

The last song on the album, "Tears for Johannesburg," reflects the cruelty experienced by the victims of the Sharpeville massacre which murdered demonstrators nonviolently protesting the laws of apartheid in South Africa.197 On March 21, 1960, anti-apartheid activism reached a peak when the Pan-Africanist Congress (PAC) organized a protest. The protest reached a devastating end when 69 of the 7,000 protestors were killed, and 186 were injured at the hands of nearly 300 police officers.198 The song reflects that there is still prejudice and violence in the world, but that there will be no giving up in the struggle for freedom. In fact, this particular song on the album was considered so dangerous by the South African government that the album was banned in the country.199 The 5/4 groove of the piece could also be viewed as a commentary on modern jazz music of the day.

At the time of the album's release in 1960, Dave Brubeck's "Take Five" had just reached peak popularity after its 1959 debut. By framing the song in such time, it could be a response to the popularity of a white jazzman's song and how a genre dominated by African-Americans still manages to be made popular by a white man. Using the 5/4 meter shows a sense of interracial competition within the jazz industry and Roach's attempt to use the beat "in a more ambitious way both musically and politically."200 Many black jazz musicians were angered by what they understood to be bias in the press, as it often overlooked some of the great jazz musicians of the African-American community, such as Roach himself.

The actual presentation of the record when it was made also speaks to its function in activism for the Civil Rights movement. The cover depicts a photograph of three black men sitting at an American diner counter, with a white man serving them.

The fact that a white man serves the three black patrons shows the visualization of the goal they are working towards.201 The *Pittsburgh Courier*, at the album's release in 1960, explained that the album was meant to be "a 'boost' for the sit-ins."202 The Sit-Ins, which had begun on February 1, 1960 in Greensboro, North Carolina, were in specific reference on the cover o f *We Insist!*, providing a link between the album's material and the modern movement.203 This action shows solidarity with the activists out on the line in the south. To show further solidarity, the album's liner notes begin with an ambitious quote by Civil Rights activist A. Philip Randolph: "A revolution is unfurling —America's unfinished revolution. It is unfurling in lunch counters, buses, libraries and schools—wherever the dignity and potential of men are denied. Youth and idealism are unfurling. Masses of Negroes are marching onto the stage of history and demanding their freedom now!"204 The fact that this is the opening note of the album shows its dedication to the message of the

Civil Rights movement. Similarly, the use of a quote by an activist with current relevance in the media shows these musicians' commitment to the cause.

At the time of the album's release, current events taking place in the American south inspired Roach and his contemporaries to respond through their art. By 1961, the Sit-In protests were in full swing throughout the southern states. Within two months, the movement "had spread to fifty-four cities in nine states and captured the imagination of racial progressives in the North and South."205 The movement, an inspiration to activists who could not be on the front lines, pushed artists such as Roach and Lincoln to express their dismay towards anti-Black prejudice and violence, continuous black cruelty and suffering, and the need for change through activism in these areas.206 The music of the Freedom Now Suite clearly exemplifies just how great a toll the violence in the south had taken on the entirety of the African-American community. The violence taking place in the American south was a continuation of the long-standing violence experienced by African Americans in United States history. The music reflects this continued violence towards African-Americans, from 100 years before its release to the present day, and provides a foil to the happy American life commonly portrayed in post-World War II media. In fact, the urgency of the Sit-In movement actually pushed the album's release to an earlier date than was originally intended. Originally meant to be released as a centennial celebration of the Emancipation Proclamation, *We Insist!* was released two years earlier than originally intended, in 1960 rather than 1962, due to the rapid progression of the Civil Rights movement.207 Before they could achieve true freedom through overturning racial prejudice, Roach and his fellow jazz musicians used their musical freedom in metaphor for "emancipation from racist restrictions."208 Jazz embodied the message of the Civil Rights movement in its emphasis on individual expression that serves a group beyond oneself—similar to how a country is made up of individuals. In order to produce a functional musical piece, each musician must work with one another and listen to the ideas of others. 209 It is this same expression of democracy that African-Americans were fighting for in their everyday lives.

With the release of *We Insist! Freedom Now Suite*, Max Roach and Abbey Lincoln brought themselves into the public sphere of activism, joining the likes of John Coltrane, Maya Angelou, and others who emphasized the importance of the Civil Rights struggle through their art. By using their art to further the movement, they will forever be remembered in the memory of the Civil Rights movement.210 Producer Nat Hentoff remembered Roach's unique view on his role in the movement: "Like the constitution, we are individual voices,' he said, 'listening intently to all the other voices and creating a whole from these personal voices."211 This speaks to the importance Roach placed on his music in the larger picture of the movement. This body of work exemplifies the African-American imagination for a better future. The *Freedom Now Suite* is also unique in its ability to communicate to the listener the distress of past generations that Lincoln felt illustrated the opposite feeling of "freedom": Lincoln's wails in "Protest" provide an image of the rapacious bullying suffered by African-Americans over the centuries. This highlights the current moment, the ongoing savagery experienced at the time of the album's release, in contrast with the experiences of African-Americans 100 years prior.212 Bassist Ron Carter discussed the link between radical political movement and jazz with his colleague Art Taylor in 1969: "Whenever there has been a major change in jazz, there's been a major change in everything else afterward....The student radicals are like the freedom jazz players who want to bypass most of the present standards for playing a tune...."213 This quote illustrates the opportunity Roach saw in his music to represent something greater than himself and his desire to involve himself in activism. Roach recognized that his fame as a jazz drummer could be put to use by making music about political issues he felt personally passionate about —specifically the Civil Rights movement.

However, Roach's idea of activism seemed to differ from that of his lyricist, Oscar Brown, Jr. During the creation of the album, the two musicians had differing ideas of how to go about expressing their political views through music that eventually led to their parting ways. Brown recalled: "...So I was preaching love. Max thought that Malcolm X had a better solution than Martin Luther King. That was the end of our dispute at the time, which was a very serious one. So that whole collaboration was aborted, and at that point it was never completed—although it was pretty near completing when we fell out."214 Whereas Martin

69

Luther King, Jr. emphasized peaceful protest as an approach to achieving racial equality, Malcolm X supported more direct action that was not necessarily non-violent.

Roach went on to claim that the NAACP had invited him to create the album for their organization, but lyricist Brown disagrees with this statement. He claimed that the original incentive to create the *Freedom Now Suite* was to "tell the story of the African drum from Africa up to contemporary times," and entitle it "The Beat."215 It was originally supposed to begin with "All Africa" before "Driva' Man," followed by "Freedom Day," to show a more "evolutionary perspective" of the music rather than assist a particular political agenda.216 Brown was disappointed to learn that Roach had altered the original order of the songs to fit his political agenda.

When asked to reflect upon the album and his relationship with Brown, Roach replied: "Oh yeah, we fought. We never could finish it. It [still] isn't finished....we don't really understand what it *really* is to be free. The last song we did, 'Freedom Day,' ended with a question mark."217 The dynamic between these two artists brought about one of the most politically charged albums of the era. Although there was bound to be disagreement, each of the musicians recognized the importance in their contribution to something that would outlive them both. Thankfully, such disagreements did not fundamentally alter the album's compositions beyond their track order in the album. Both Brown and Roach understood the influence the album could have on the movement towards racial equality in America, regardless of the means used to get there. The music of *We Insist!* Uses manifestations of African-American cultural identity, in blues, jazz, and spiritual verses, to connect with audiences involved with the Civil Rights movement, African nationalism, and the Sharpeville massacre to show there is an interconnectedness between people of African heritage around the world.218

Roach and Lincoln also used the album in order to fundraise for various Civil Rights organizations throughout the 1960s by donating the profits of the album as well as playing it at various benefit concerts. As Dizzy Gillespie stated: "Jazz musicians don't have no money, so they can't pay off stations to play it. Jazz is the only thing we have to offer the world."219 Therefore, Roach and Lincoln used benefit concerts such as the 52nd annual convention of the NAACP, or at the Village Gate for Congress for Racial Equality (CORE), to raise money for the Civil Rights movement. The first time the album was performed was on January 15, 1961 at an event sponsored by CORE at New York's Village Gate.220 Lincoln astonished local audiences with her eccentric performance consisting of screams and sighs beyond merely lyrics.221 The event had been set up by fellow CORE member Jimmy McDonald, a folksinger himself, who presented the event in collaboration with other socially aware artists such as Maya Angelou, who danced during the performance, and actress and activist Ruby Dee, who narrated and gave the performance a more specific context. The live performance differed from the recorded version as it did not include

Coleman Hawkins, but did include Max Roach on drums, trumpeter Booker Little on trumpet, trumpeter Marcus Belgrave, trombonist Julian Priester, alto saxophonist Eric Dolphy, tenor saxophonist Walter Benton, drummer Michael Olatunji and four conga drummers, bassist Larry Ridley, and singer Abbey Lincoln.222 The poster advertising the event depicted the same photograph as the album cover, referencing the Sit-In movement once again.223

Max Roach's and Abbey Lincoln's collaborative work *We Insist! Freedom Now Suite* exemplifies the struggle faced by African-Americans in a racist American society for the last 100 years. An homage to such a struggle, the album's five songs reflects the passion and dedication of its contributors, Max Roach, Abbey Lincoln, Oscar Brown, Jr., Michael Olatunji, and Coleman Hawkins, to the movement towards racial equality. Its poignant references to the violence faced by African-Americans on American soil as well as in South Africa makes the album hold political significance in its message. Furthermore, the use of the album to raise money for various Civil Rights organizations, such as CORE and NAACP, through benefit concerts or record sales illustrates the contribution of the album to the movement beyond simply artistic significance. Lastly, the album's artwork of both black and white men together exemplifies the goal of racial equality that its creators hoped for.

Conclusion

Ultimately, jazz music contributed greatly to the Civil Rights movement. As the majority of jazz musicians during the mid-twentieth century were African-American, it is no wonder that the struggle for racial equality permeated the genre. The discrimination faced by these musicians was incentive to act in favor of equal rights for all races, and they brought this attitude into their music as well. The racial prejudice experienced by these musicians was evident in all areas of the industry. Especially after World War II, winning the "Double Victory" campaign—freedom abroad as well as racial freedom at home—was on the forefront of everyone's mind. Unfortunately, African-Americans returned home only to find that they were returning to the same world from which they had left.

Thus, musicians looked to change the problem of racial prejudice in jazz and beyond. One of the driving factors for racial equality in the jazz industry was economics. Many Black jazz musicians were poorly affected by the issue of the cabaret card in New York City, which restricted musicians from playing in specific venues and increased competitiveness. Moreover, many were unable to afford the same opportunities given to their White counterparts, such as the ability to open up their own club. The majority of venues played by Black musicians were owned by Whites and attended by exclusively White audiences. Jim Crow came to influence the genre over the decades.

The audience was originally comprised of exclusively African-Americans and became more interracial as the century progressed. The musicians, similarly were originally exclusively African-American and attracted more White musicians towards the middle of the twentieth century. African-American musicians faced extremely difficult conditions when traveling in the United States, such as not being able to find satisfactory housing on tour or not being allowed to dine in the same place they may be performing that night. Oftentimes, the Black community would supply these necessities for the musicians so that they may keep sharing their music on tour.

However, the experience of the traveling African-American musician was oftentimes extremely different abroad. Black musicians were regarded highly and were greatly appreciated by the audiences they visited. The United States' decision to sponsor African-Americans abroad was ironic in that these musicians were treated so poorly back home, but still were asked to represent the United States abroad. Musicians such as Louis Armstrong, Dizzy Gillespie, amongst others, spread jazz throughout the world on the U.S. Ambassador Tours from the mid-1950s to the late 1970s. Although this may have projected a false representation of race relations in the United States, these artists used their celebrity status abroad to bring attention to the struggle for equal rights at home. The work of these musicians brought together a diverse array of people across the world to hear the United States' message of democracy, but also to spread awareness of the Civil Rights movement and the struggle for these musicians to exercise their basic democratic rights in their home country.

Jazz musicians also had various perspectives on how to handle racial prejudice. Some were much more outspoken than others. For example, Thelonious Monk was rather apolitical in his stance on racial equality. However, this does not mean that he did not support the cause. The importance of the Civil Rights movement moved rather apolitical musicians, such as Monk, to involve themselves in the best way they felt comfortable.

Oftentimes, this was through participation in benefit concerts. The various concerts sponsored by Civil Rights organizations attracted some of the greatest names in jazz at the time. By associating themselves with these organizations, these musicians show that they supported the movement despite their lack of public vocalization.

On the other hand, more publicly vocal artists also used jazz music to express their views on the Civil Rights movement. The Civil Rights movement inspired Max Roach and Abbey Lincoln to exhibit this dedication in their album, *We Insist!: Freedom Now Suite.* Even the album's cover artwork, depicting three African-American men at a diner counter served by a White man, speaks to the Civil Rights struggle. More specifically, the cover references the Sit-In movement of Greensboro, North Carolina in 1960, which began shortly before the album's release. The album not only shows solidarity with the southern activists on the front line, but also references the struggle of African-Americans over the past century. The music reflects the long-standing violence experienced by African-Americans, from slavery to present-day. The album's release date was even moved to an earlier release date than was originally intended in order to show greater support for the movement.

Furthermore, *We Insist!: Freedom Now Suite* was first played at a benefit concert sponsored by CORE at New York's Village Gate. The concert drew the attention of Maya Angelou, a poet who danced during the performance, as well as Ruby Dee, an actress who narrated the performance for context. Due to union laws, musicians were required to be paid a minimum for all performances. However, musicians participating in such concerts would often donate all proceeds to the organizations, further showing their solidarity with the Civil Rights movement. The effort of the musicians, who oftentimes were already struggling to find work, to raise money for the cause shows the importance and emphasis placed on the effort towards racial equality in the United States. Roach and Lincoln exemplified the importance of this issue in their album, and went on to even release it free of cost for any Civil Rights organization who may want to use it.

Jazz ultimately embodied the principles of the Civil Rights movement in its democratic structure and freedom to express oneself. The music itself reflected the change in political consciousness that affected these artists. Their unconventional and ever-changing attitude towards the music during the Civil Rights era reflected their objection to the idea of racial inequality as they strove to garner respect for themselves as well as their music by the American public. These musicians recognized the ability of jazz to bring people together across the color line, as well as its ability to celebrate the individual within a larger collective. Although a jazz band may be constituted of multiple individual musician, each has the opportunity to solo and add to the conservatory aspect of jazz during each performance.

The bandstand was one of the first places in the United States these musicians experienced the breaking down of the color line. By taking this music abroad as well as publicizing it at home, jazz artists showed the world that racial equality is possible. The bandstand was a place of freedom: one that these artists hoped would serve as a precursor for the rest of the country. Black and White musicians could play side by side, with mutual respect for what each had to offer for the music. A result of the melting pot of various different cultures, jazz embodied the democratic ideals of the United States. These musicians hoped, through their music, to bring these ideals to the African-American community.

Bibliography

Baraka, Amiri. "The Great Max Roach." In *Digging: The Afro-American Soul of American Classical Music*, 214-18. Music of the African Diaspora. Berkeley, CA: University of California Press, 2009.

Bohlman, Philip V., and Goffredo Plastino, eds. *Jazz Worlds/World Jazz*. Chicago, IL: The University of Chicago Press, 2016.

Castledine, Jacqueline. "Gender, Jazz, and Justice in Cold War Freedom Movements." In *Freedom Rights: New Perspectives on the Civil Rights Movement*, edited by Danielle L. McGuire and John Dittmer, 223-46. Lexington, KY: University Press of Kentucky, 2011.

Chinen, Nate. *Playing Changes: Jazz for the New Century* Toronto: Pantheon Books, 2018.

Cooks, Bridget R., and Graham Eng-Wilmot. "Sound of the Break: Jazz and the Failures of Emancipation." *American Quarterly* 68, no. 2 (June 2016): 315-40. Project MUSE.

Davenport, Lisa. "The Paradox of Jazz Diplomacy: Race and Culture in the Cold War." In *African Americans in U.S. Foreign Policy: From the Era of Frederick Douglass to the Age of Obama*, edited by Linda Heywood, Allison Blakely, Charles Stith, and Joshua C. Yesnowitz, 140-74. Champaign, IL: University of Illinois Press, 2015. Digital file.

Footnotes

1 Robin D. G. Kelley, *Thelonious Monk: The Life and Times of an American Original* (New York, NY: Free Press, 2009), 164.

2 Ibid., 57.

3 Ingrid Monson, *Freedom Sounds: Civil Rights Call Out to Jazz and Africa* (Oxford University Press, 2007), 7, digital file.

4 Ibid., 31.

5 Kelley, Thelonious Monk, 108.

6 Travelers' Green Book: 1966-67 *International Edition: For Vacation Without Aggravation* (New York, NY: Victor H. Green & Co., 1966), 87, accessed April 16, 2019, https://digitalcollections.nypl.org/items/27516920-8308-0132-5063-58d385a7bbd0/boo k#page/26/mode/1up.

7 Christopher Gair, *American Counterculture* (Edinburgh, Scotland: Edinburgh University Press, 2007), 64.

8 Burton W. Peretti, *Jazz In American Culture*, The American Ways Series (Chicago, IL: Ivan R. Dee, 1997), 117.

9 Monson, *Freedom Sounds*, 33.

10 Ibid., 281.

11 Ibid., 78.

12 Kelley, *Thelonious Monk*, 417.

13 Monson, Freedom Sounds, 64.

14 Ibid. 1

5 LeRoi Jones, *Blues People: Negro Music in White*

America (New York City, NY: William Morrow and Company, 1963), 186.

16 Ibid., 184-185.

17 Kelley, *Thelonious Monk*, 107.

18 Ibid., 374. 1

9 Monson, *Freedom Sounds*, 186-187.

20 Gair, *American Counterculture*, 64.

21 Kelley, *Thelonious Monk*, 107.

22 Gair, *American Counterculture*, 64.

23 Jones, *Blues People*, 210.

24 Ibid., 219.

25 Ibid.

26 Ibid.

27 Monson, *Freedom Sounds*, 69-70.

28 Nathaniel Mackey, "Other: From Noun to Verb," *Representations* 39 (Summer 1992): 51.

29 Kelley, *Thelonious Monk*, 354.

30 Ibid.

31 Ibid., 355.

32 Ibid.

33 Ibid.

34 Ibid.

35 Ibid., 356.

36 Ibid.

38 Monson, *Freedom Sounds*, 223.

39 Nat Hentoff, *At the Jazz Band Ball: Sixty Years on the Jazz Scene* (Berkeley, CA: University of California Press, 2010), 115.

40 Kelley, *Thelonious Monk*, 58.

41 Jones, *Blues People*, 177.

42 Monson, *Freedom Sounds*, 80.

43 Ira Gitler, *Swing to Bop: An Oral History of the*

Transition in Jazz in the 1940s (Oxford, England: Oxford University Press, 1985), 307, digital file.

44 Monson, *Freedom Sounds*, 37.

45 Kelley, *Thelonious Monk*, 91.

46 Gitler, *Swing to Bop*, 304.

47 Ibid., 107.

48 Clark Halker, "A History of Local 208 and the Struggle for Racial Equality in the American Federation of Musicians," *Black Music Research Journal* 8, no. 2 (Fall 1988): 207.

49 Kelley, *Thelonious Monk*, 232.

50 *Monson*, Freedom Sounds, 65.

51 Jones, *Blues People*, 200.

52 Kelley, *Thelonious Monk*, 289.

53 Gitler, *Swing to Bop*, 303.

54 Nate Chinen, *Playing Changes: Jazz for the New Century* (Toronto: Pantheon Books, 2018), 6.

55 Jason Robinson, "The Challenge of the Changing Same: The Jazz Avant-garde of the 1960s, the Black Aesthetic, and the Black Arts Movement," *Critical Studies in Improvisation* 1, no. 2 (2013): 26.

56 Eric Porter, "Practicing 'Creative Music' The Black Arts Imperative in the Jazz Community," in *What Is This Thing Called Jazz?: African American Musi* California Press, 2002), 192, digital file.

57 Barack Obama, "Remarks" (speech, White House International Jazz Day Concert, Washington, DC, April 29, 2016).

58 Gair, *American Counterculture*, 65.

59 Chinen, *Playing Changes*, 65.

60 Ibid., 132.

61 Ibid., 240.

62 Monson, *Freedom Sounds*, 28.

63 Kelley, *Thelonious Monk*, 199.

64 Gitler, *Swing to Bop*, 311.

65 Kelley, *Thelonious Monk*, 316.

66 Gitler, *Swing to Bop*, 303.

67 Monson, *Freedom Sounds*, 12.

68 Ibid., 206.

69 Ibid., 160.

70 Ibid., 219.

71 Ralph Ellison, "The World and the Jug," 1964, in *The Collected Essays of Ralph Ellison: Revised and Updated* (New York, NY: Random House, 1995), 183.

72 Monson, *Freedom Sounds*, 6.

73 Porter, "Practicing 'Creative." 198.

74 Monson, *Freedom Sounds*, 12.

75 Ibid., 70.

76 Ibid., 160.

About the author:

Christa Gammage is a native New Yorker who lives in
Brooklyn with her cat Lola. She enjoys yoga and spending
time with her friends. Two of her greatest passions are music
and American history. *Freedom Now! The Function of Jazz
in the Civil Rights Movement* is her first book.

Made in the USA
Las Vegas, NV
27 January 2024

84940249R00049